JAMES BOND

The name's Bond, James Bond, but you can call him 007. When it comes to all-action adventure, this super cool spy guy is licensed to thrill!

REAL INSPIRATION

James Bond was created in the 1950s by the novelist Ian Fleming. During the Second World War, Fleming had worked for British Naval Intelligence and learned lots of spy secrets. He based the character of 007 on two real-life spies – a British hero named Sidney Reilly and a daring double agent called Dusko Popov.

BOND, THE BIRD-WATCHER

Ian Fleming named his character after one of his neighbours – who preferred bird-watching to saving the world!

GADGETS AND GIZMOS

The equipment used by spies is never what it seems. What at first glance looks like an everyday object, on closer inspection turns out to have a secret spy function...

SPIES QUIZ

What name does the CIA give to spy gadgets?

a) sneakers
b) sneakies
c) tweakies

What did agents in the Second World War hide in cigarette lighters?

a) cigarettes
b) maps
c) compasses

What were small spy cameras called?

a) minicameras
b) pinhole cameras
c) microcameras

(answers on page 32)

GET IN THE Q

Before setting off on a mission, James Bond always visits an inventor code-named 'Q' to pick up the latest spy gadget. Q's character was based on a real person named Charles Fraser-Smith (1904-92) who designed top-secret spy equipment for British secret agents during the Second World War.

SECRET COMPARTMENTS

Coins, pens and even golf balls have been designed with hidden compartments for concealing secret documents. During the Second World War, some British agents were armed with hairbrushes! Although they looked ordinary, these brushes had been designed by Charles Fraser-Smith and contained a secret drawer for hiding maps and photographs.

SPIES   TIVES

by **Hazel Poole**

9. L. RING

Contents

Clever Clogs Books
Copyright © 2006 *ticktock* Entertainment Ltd.
http://www.ticktock.co.uk

PURE GOLD

Casino Royale was the 21st Bond film to be produced, and introduced Daniel Craig as 007, making him the sixth actor to play James Bond. The film is based on the first book that Ian Fleming wrote about the spy with a licence to kill.

Pierce Brosna[n]

BOND IS BIG

The 12 original Bond books written by Ian Fleming have sold over 18 million copies worldwide and 007 has appeared in no less than 20 action-packed films. According to the latest estimates, half the world's population has seen a Bond film.

Scene from *Goldfinger*

BOND BADDIES

As well as many fans, Bond has many enemies! They include the likes of Auric Goldfinger, the evil mastermind behind a plan to steal the Federal gold reserves – seen here about to cut 007 in half with a laser beam. Goldfinger is assisted by his bodyguard and henchman Oddjob. As well as being a martial arts expert, Oddjob is also armed with a hat that, when thrown, can slice the head off a stone statue!

The world's smallest phone 'bug' (used for secretly listening to other peoples' calls) has been nicknamed the 'rice grain' by spies. That's because, at just 10 mm long, it's no bigger than a grain of rice!

SECRET WEAPONS

Everyday things can also be adapted to hide weapons. In 1978, a Bulgarian writer named Georgi Markov was murdered in London by a foreign spy. He was killed by a tiny pellet of poison that was jabbed into his leg using the tip of a deadly umbrella.

IN THE PICTURE

Take a good look at this ring. Smile, please! Despite its ordinary appearance, the ring actually contains a tiny camera. The black spot in the centre of the ring is the camera lens. It belonged to a real-life Russian spy and was used for taking secret photographs.

Spy camera

Coin concealing microfilm

SPIES QUIZ

Where was Mata Hari born?

a) Swaziland
b) Holland
c) Paris

Belle Boyd was a famous spy during which war?

a) First World War
b) US Civil War
c) American War
   of Independence

By what name was spy Marthe Richer known?

a) L'Alouette
b) Tokyo Rose
c) Tiger Eyes

(answers on page 32)

QUEEN OF DISGUISES

Annette Kerner was one of the greatest ever real-life private eyes. Known as the 'Queen of Disguises', she could transform her appearance to suit any situation. She even posed as a waitress in a café used by criminals so that she could eavesdrop on their conversation. One of her most daring adventures involved disguising herself as a drug addict to capture a gang of opium dealers.

Annette Kerner

THE PRICE YOU PAY

Mata Hari tried to find out useful information from her many admirers then secretly passed it onto the German Secret Service. Eventually, she was betrayed and captured by the French. The penalty if you are caught spying is often death. Mata Hari's case was no exception, and in 1917 she was sent before the firing squad.

LIP SERVICE

The Supercircuits Model PL51XP is a spy video camera small enough to fit in a tube of lipstick. It can beam live pictures up to 150 m away!

WOMEN SPIES AND PRIVATE EYES

If you think all spies are men, think again. Many women have become undercover agents, too. These female sleuths and snoops were no strangers to daring exploits...

Mata Hari

WOMEN AT WAR

During the Second World War, Britain's elite Special Operations Executive (SOE) recruited and trained many women spies. These women were given false papers and identities and were dropped behind enemy lines in France. Their job was to gather information, organise undercover sabotage operations and help British soldiers avoid being captured.

THE DANCING SPY

One of the most famous female spies was a dancer known as 'Mata Hari', although her real name was Margaretha Geertruida Zelle. During the First World War she lived in France and many important people came to see her show. But secretly, Mata Hari was watching them just as closely as they were watching her!

EYE IN THE SKY

The latest spy planes and satellites give secret agents a brilliant bird's-eye view. But when it comes to espionage, the sky is **NOT** the limit – there are spies under the oceans, too.

SPIES QUIZ

What is the name of the F-117A Stealth fighter?

a) *Blackbird*
b) *Nightshade*
c) *Nighthawk*

Why must pilots wear spacesuits when flying the Lockheed SR-71?

a) to keep out draughts
b) to disguise themselves
c) to stop their blood from boiling

What is the newly-launched spy satellite called?

a) *Early Bird*
b) *Spysat I*
c) *Skywatch*

(answers on page 32)

WE HAVE LIFT OFF

Even space is used for spying! Top-secret spy satellites can detect the launch of missiles and provide early warning of an enemy attack. They can also track the movement of soldiers, ships and tanks – and beam photographs of them back down to Earth.

INVISIBLE PAINT

Most planes show up on radar screens but the F-117A fighter plane is coated with a special black paint that absorbs radar signals. It also has radar-jamming equipment on board. As a result, the plane is almost impossible to detect – just the job for secret spying missions!

FAST MOVER

The US Air Force's Lockheed SR-71 is the ultimate spy plane. Not only is it the fastest jet plane in the world with a top speed of more than 3,500 km/h, it can also reach an altitude of almost 30,000 metres – that's more than twice as high as most other planes can go!

Lockheed SR-71

IN THE PICTURE

The most powerful spy satellite is capable of photographing something as small as a crossword puzzle from a distance of more than 200 km!

IN DEEP WATER

Sleeping Beauty

As well as spies in the sky, there are spies deep below the waves, too. This tiny submarine, known as *Sleeping Beauty*, was used by secret agents during the Second World War. It was so small and quiet that it could creep up close to the enemy without being noticed.

9

SPIES QUIZ

The most frequently used letter in the English alphabet is...

a) T
b) A
c) E

What is cryptography?

a) the study of crypts
b) the decoding of messages
c) a type of shorthand

Which of the following did Samuel Morse also invent?

a) the telegraph
b) the telephone
c) the radio

(answers on page 32)

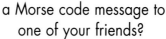

The Morse Code

A	• –	S	• • •
B	– • • •	T	–
C	– • – •	U	• • –
D	– • •	V	• • • –
E	•	W	• – –
F	• • – •	X	– • • –
G	– – •	Y	– • – –
H	• • • •	Z	– – • •
I	• •	1	• – – – –
J	• – – –	2	• • – – –
K	– • –	3	• • • – –
L	• – • •	4	• • • • –
M	– –	5	• • • • •
N	– •	6	– • • • •
O	– – –	7	– – • • •
P	• – – •	8	– – – • •
Q	– – • –	9	– – – – •
R	• – •	0	– – – – –

COMPLETELY DOTTY

The most famous code of all is called Morse Code. It's named after Samuel Morse, the man who invented it in 1840. It was used to send messages by telegraph. Each letter of the alphabet is represented by a series of dots and dashes. How about sending a Morse code message to one of your friends?

STICK AT IT

One of the oldest ways of sending a secret message was to wind a long, thin piece of paper around a stick. The message was written horizontally along the stick and then unwound, making the letters appear all jumbled up. To read the message, the paper was simply wound back around the stick.

An Enigma machine

10

CODE-CRACKER

Spies use secret codes when sending messages. This way, even if a message falls into the wrong hands, enemies won't be able to work out what it means.

WHAT AN ENIGMA

During the Second World War, German spies sent secret messages using a code called Enigma. To put a message into code they used a special keyboard like the one in the picture. What the Germans didn't realize was that a team of Polish mathmaticians had cracked the code a year before the war started!

LISTEN UP

Between 1955 and 1961, British and American spies secretly listened to more than 443,000 phone calls in East Germany – a world record for eavesdropping!

GET CRACKING!

Secret codes are nothing new. Spies have been using them to send messages for hundreds of years. In fact, the first book about codes, explaining how to make them up and crack them, was published back in 1379.

SPY DISGUISE

If you want to be a spy you must learn how to keep your real identity a secret and observe people without them noticing who you are. To do this, you must become a master of disguise!

FRUIT-FUL IDEAS

Fresh lemon juice makes great invisible ink. When the juice dries, your message will disappear.
To make it reappear, simply hold the piece of paper under a hair dryer.

Everyday clothes
An elaborate outfit will only attract attention – the last thing a spy wants to do!

Dark glasses and hat
These help to hide the agent's face so he can't be recognised.

Electronic notepad
To record observations.

Binoculars
For observing people at a safe distance.

DESPERATE MEASURES

It's not just spies who are concerned about disguising their appearance. Some criminals will also go to great lengths to avoid being recognised. An outlaw named Ritchie Ramos, for instance, spent £45,000 on plastic surgery while on the run from police in America!

LADIES AND GENTLEMEN

One of the most daring and successful disguises was employed by a French spy known as the Chevalier d'Eon. While working as a British double agent, he disguised himself as a woman in order to gain the trust of the Empress of Russia. The disguise was so successful that no one knew he was actually a man until he died in 1810!

Mobile phone
To stay in touch with friendly agents.

Backpack
For carrying other equipment (such as a camera), plus some different clothes – just in case the spy needs to quickly change appearance.

TOP TIP

A newspaper is one accessory that no good spy should ever be without. It gives you something to pretend to read while you are secretly watching something (or someone) else. What's more, when you hold it up in front of your face, other people can't see what you look like.

SPIES QUIZ

Who was known as the 'Ace of Spies'?

a) James Bond
b) Sidney Reilly
c) Guy Burgess

Who became President Lincoln's spymaster?

a) Allan Pinkerton
b) Robert Baden-Powell
c) Bill Howard-Bailey

What is the name of Rudyard Kipling's spy novel?

a) *If*
b) *Kim*
c) *The Jungle Book*

(answers on page 32)

DOUBLE AGENTS

A double agent is a spy who has secretly changed sides. His old friends still think he is working for them when in fact he is passing on all their secrets to the enemy. This makes a double agent doubly dangerous!

MOLES AND BUGS

A mole is a spy who works for an enemy organisation to gain access to secret information. A bug is spy slang for a hidden microphone used for listening in on other people's conversations.

DEAD LETTER BOX

A dead letter box (or DLB for short) is a place where spies can secretly leave messages for each other or collect them. In the 1980s, the KGB (the former Soviet Union's secret spy organisation) used a marble column in a London church as a DLB. A small blue mark on a lamppost outside the church showed agents that a message was waiting to be collected. A white mark on a bench nearby meant the message had been picked up.

A secret DLB?

SPY LINGO

If you really want to get to grips with the cloak-and-dagger world of espionage, you'll have to learn some of the slang spies use...

SPYMASTER

A senior spy who is in charge of other secret ~~...~~ often known as a spymaster. This photograph shows a spymaster called Markus Wolf – known as 'the man without a face' because for many years no one knew what he looked like. Wolf worked for the East German Secret Police and was responsible for organising spying operations in foreign countries.

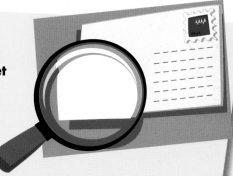

MICRODOT **During the Second World War, German spies sent secret documents to each other by shrinking them to 1/400th of their original size. Known as microdots, they were small enough to be hidden on the edge of a postcard!**

SPIES AGAINST CRIMES

Not all agents spy on foreign countries. Some are busy
closer to home fighting crime – and spying on other spies!

GIMME MI5

Like many other countries, the UK has two intelligence
organisations. While MI6 is responsible for international
espionage, agents working for MI5 deal with counter-
intelligence – stopping spies from other countries
discovering British secrets. MI5 also helps
the police to catch criminals.

FBI AND CIA

In the USA, MI6's job is done
by the Central Intelligence
Agency (or CIA for short),
while the Federal Bureau
of Investigation (FBI) has
a similar role to MI5.
The FBI has 58 offices
throughout America
and its agents (like
Mulder and Scully
in the *X-files*) are
specially trained to
tackle serious crimes,
including bank robbery
and kidnapping.

Mulder and Scully

THE SPY NEXT DOOR

East Germany had more spies than any other country. Most were ordinary people who were encouraged to spy on their neighbours. By 1985, one in every 50 people living there was a spy!

TOP SECRET

MI5 was formed in 1909 – although its activities were so secret that the government didn't officially admit it existed until 1989! Agents working for MI5 have the power to investigate anyone who might threaten the UK's national security.

SECRET FILES

Security organisations such as MI5 and the CIA hold intelligence files on known criminals and foreign spies. These files contain details of where they live, where they like to go, the names they use and all other kinds of useful information!

SPIES QUIZ

In 1992, Stella Rimington became the first woman to head which Western intelligence agency?

a) FBI
b) MI6
c) MI5

Who headed the FBI from 1924-1972?

a) J. Edgar Hoover
b) Richard Nixon
c) Harry Palmer

What does 'MI' in MI5 stand for?

a) Military Intelligence
b) Major Investigator
c) we can't tell you – it's top secret!

(answers on page 32)

Spy files

AN EYE ON THE WORLD

SPIES QUIZ

How many countries are there in Interpol?

a) 500
b) 125
c) 177

Interpol was formed...

a) after the First World War
b) after the Second World War
c) during the Cold War

Where in France are Interpol's headquarters?

a) Paris
b) Lyon
c) Rouen

(answers on page 32)

Crime is an international problem. To tackle the biggest criminal operations, police forces in different countries must work together. And that's where Interpol comes in...

INTERNATIONAL RESCUE

The International Criminal Police Organisation (known as 'Interpol' for short) was formed in 1923. It is made up of police forces from many different countries. Interpol enables different police organisations to share information, such as fingerprint records. It's a major weapon in the fight against organised crime around the world.

Marijuana

GET OUT OF BED OR DIE!

The most severe law maker was an ancient Greek called Draco. In 621 BC, he made almost every crime punishable by execution – even laziness!

MONEY, MONEY, MONEY!

Drug-smuggling is big business. In 1989, following a long undercover surveillance operation, police in the USA pounced on a gang of international smugglers and seized drugs worth around £4.4 billion.

THE MAFIA MOB

The world's largest and most famous criminal organisation is known as the Mafia. It is thought to be involved in criminal activity all over the world and employs around 5,000 people. Every year, its illegal operations make a profit of more than £50 billion – that's more money than most international companies make!

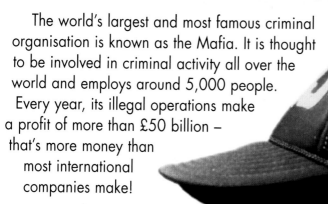

TEAM WORK

A good example of different police forces working together happened in 1982. In a combined operation between the US Drug Enforcement Agency and the Colombian Police, no less than 495 people were arrested for smuggling a drug called marijuana, made from the hemp plant.

CRIME BOSS CAPONE

In 1919, alcohol was outlawed in America. This provided gangsters with the perfect opportunity to make money by bootlegging (selling alcohol illegally). Al Capone ran the bootlegging operation in the city of Chicago and defended his territory fiercely. It is thought that he was involved in more than 1,000 murders.

SPIES QUIZ

Who played Eliot Ness in the film *The Untouchables*?

a) Sean Connery
b) Tom Cruise
c) Kevin Costner

By what name was Al Capone also known as?

a) Scarface
b) The Godfather
c) The Boss

What was the name of Britain's first police force?

a) Bobbies
b) Peelers
c) Rattlers

(answers on page 32)

WHAT A RACKET

The first detectives to patrol the streets of London carried rattles in their coat-tails. When they were chasing a criminal, they would wave the rattle to raise the alarm.

THE UNTOUCHABLES

In the early part of this century, a great detective hero appeared in America. His name was Eliot Ness and he was responsible for finally putting the gangster Al Capone behind bars. Ness and his team became known as the 'Untouchables' because they would not be bribed or bullied by criminals.

EARLY DETECTIVES

The earliest crime-busters really had their work cut out – and nowhere more so than in the USA, where vicious gangsters made sure there was trouble!

A US sheriff

EYE SAY!

The oldest private detective agency in the world was set up by an American named Allan Pinkerton back in 1850. And it's still going strong today. Its trademark is an open eye – which gave rise to the name 'private eye', meaning a private detective.

STAR SHERIFF

In the USA, the person in charge of law enforcement in a county is called a sheriff. Usually, the sheriff wears a badge with a six-pointed star. Allan Pinkerton began his career as a US sheriff and brought several notorious Wild West outlaws to justice – including a gang of train robbers called the Reno brothers. He also uncovered a plot to assassinate Abraham Lincoln, the US president! at that time.

BACK FROM THE DEAD

With his trademark pipe and deerstalker hat, Sherlock Holmes quickly became very popular. Then, in 1893, Conan Doyle decided to write a story in which Holmes was killed. The detective's fans were furious. In fact, the public outcry was so great that Conan Doyle had to write another story to bring Holmes back to life!

FACT NOT FICTION

Sir Arthur Conan Doyle was a real-life amateur detective and actually helped to solve several crimes.

CHRISTIE'S CHARACTERS

The author Agatha Christie came up with not one but two great detective characters – a little, white-haired old lady called Miss Marple, and a fussy Frenchman with a curly moustache named Hercule Poirot. All of Christie's murder mysteries are famous for the clever twists in their plots – the murderer is always the person you least expect it to be!

James Coco as Hercule Poirot

FICTIONAL DETECTIVES

The first detective story ever written was by an author called Edgar Allen Poe and featured a crime-busting supersleuth named C. Auguste Dupin. He is now over 150 years old!

PARTNERS IN CRIME

The most famous detective character of all is Sherlock Holmes. More than 200 films have been made of his adventures – making him the most portrayed character of all time. Holmes and his trusty companion, Dr Watson, were created by the British novelist Sir Arthur Conan Doyle who wrote no less than 68 detective stories.

EAGLE EYES

Conan Doyle based the character of Holmes partly on a real person called Joseph Bell. Bell was a doctor who became famous for working out what was wrong with his patients by observing them very closely. It was exactly this kind of eagle-eye observation that enabled Holmes to solve some of his most baffling cases.

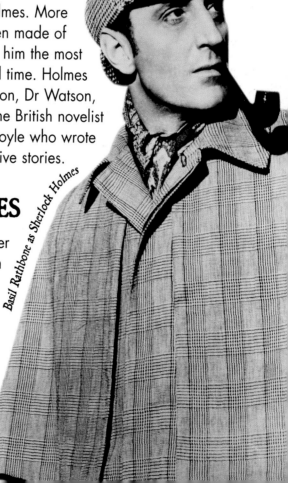

Basil Rathbone as Sherlock Holmes

DOG DETECTIVES

Our four-legged friends have been helping the police catch criminals since the 1800s. With such smart police dogs about, crooks had better watch out - especially cat burglars!

ON THE SCENT

The first dogs used for detective work were bloodhounds. With their super-sensitive noses, they can follow the scent of an outlaw on the run – even if there is no trace of footprints. In fact, once they get a whiff of a villain, bloodhounds have been known to follow their noses for more than 80 km.

NOT TO BE SNIFFED AT

Dog's noses are one million times more powerful than human noses. Only eels and butterflies are better at sniffing things out!

DRESSED FOR THE JOB

Police dogs in some forces even have their own special uniforms! These include bulletproof vests, boots to protect the dog's paws and a special harness containing a video camera which can be attached to the dog's head.

TOUGH TRAINING

a German shepherd in training

Most police dogs these days are German shepherds or labradors. Before they join the force they must pass a tough 14-week basic training course. Only pups that make the grade go on to learn advanced skills, like how to sniff out drugs and explosives or disarm someone with a gun.

TOP DOG

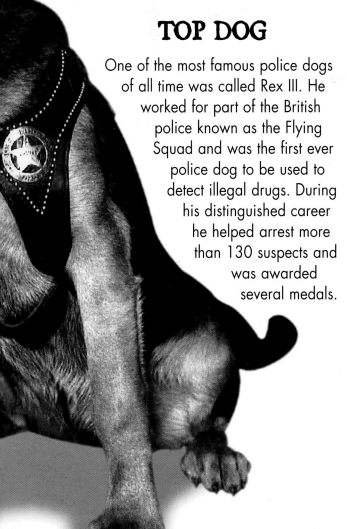

One of the most famous police dogs of all time was called Rex III. He worked for part of the British police known as the Flying Squad and was the first ever police dog to be used to detect illegal drugs. During his distinguished career he helped arrest more than 130 suspects and was awarded several medals.

SPIES QUIZ

What is a German shepherd dog also known as?

a) a Labrador
b) an Alsatian
c) a Rottweiler

What are dog teams sometimes called?

a) canine teams
b) K-9s
c) a dog brigade

What cartoon dog detective has a partner called Shaggy?

a) Lassie
b) Scrappy
c) Scooby Doo

(answers on page 32)

POINTING THE FINGER

The tiny grooves on the tips of your fingers leave fingerprints on everything you touch. Everyone's fingerprints are different, which means they can be used to identify who you are. The FBI currently has 173 million sets of fingerprints in its records – the largest collection in the world!

A loop fingerprint

9. L. RING

SPIES QUIZ

How many blood groups are there?

a) 3
b) 4
c) 5

What is the DNA structure known as?

a) double helix
b) double whammy
c) chromosome twist

Loop, arch and compound – which type of fingerprint is missing?

a) wheel
b) whirl
c) whorl

(answers on page 32)

NOW AND THEN

Detectives started looking for fingerprints back in the 1800s. In the late nineteenth century, a British policeman called Edward Henry classified fingerprints into four different groups and gave each one a name. Nowadays, computers make short work of finding a matching pair of prints – making crime-busting even quicker.

GOT IT LICKED

It's not just your fingerprints or DNA that are unique. Like your fingers, your tongue is covered in a pattern of grooves and no two people have exactly the same tongueprint, either!

26

SCENE OF THE CRIME

When they get to the scene of a crime, detectives start looking for clues. One thing they are really hoping to find is a fingerprint.

PERSONAL BAR CODES

By taking a sample of body tissue (such as blood, hair or skin) found at the scene of a crime, police scientists can create what's called a 'DNA fingerprint'. It looks a bit like the bar codes you see printed on things in shops. They can then compare this with the DNA of their suspects. A match can often be used to prove whether someone is innocent or guilty.

A model of DNA cells

MAGIC MOLECULE

Every cell in your body contains something called deoxyribonucleic acid, known as DNA for short. DNA is complicated stuff – as this model shows! It's our DNA that makes us who we are and no two people have exactly the same DNA. Which is good news for detectives. To find out why, keep reading...

CLOSING THE TRAP

Once detectives have identified their suspect, they set about gathering enough evidence to prove that this person is guilty. Here's how!

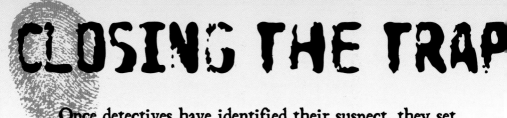

WITNESS STATEMENTS

Detectives spend time talking to witnesses and checking out the suspect's alibi (what they claim they were doing or who they were with when the crime happened). Each witness is carefully interviewed and their words are written down as a statement for use in court during a trial.

A bugging device

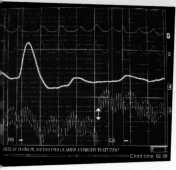

A polygraph

THE WHOLE TRUTH?

Lie detectors (or polygraphs) measure tiny changes in a suspect's blood pressure, heartbeat and breathing as he or she answers questions. This information can be used as a guide to tell whether or not the person is telling the truth. The results appear on a graph, like the one above. The polygraph was first used in 1924.

ON THE RIGHT TRACK

Tracking devices, known as bumper beepers, can be secretly attached to cars so that police can follow their every move. The bleeper is actually a tiny radio transmitter which sends out an electronic signal wherever it goes. This allows detectives to follow the car from a safe distance, unseen.

SPIES QUIZ

What is another name for a post-mortem?

a) an autoplasty
b) an autopsy
c) a biopsy

What is the BBC's crime investigation programme called?

a) *TV Detectives*
b) *Police Files*
c) *Crimewatch UK*

Who was the first criminal to be caught thanks to a radio message?

a) Dr. Crippen
b) the Boston Strangler
c) Jack the Ripper

(answers on page 32)

STOP BUGGING ME!

Tiny hidden microphones, called bugs, are sometimes installed in a suspect's home so detectives can listen in to what this person says. Some microphones, like the one in the picture, are small enough to be hidden behind a picture or under a table without anyone noticing.

SPIES QUIZ

What is a scrambler?

a) a type of lie detector
b) a device for keeping calls private
c) a machine used for writing secret code

What is the illegal copying of videos or CDs called?

a) piracy
b) duplicity
c) mastering

The average European annual losses through audio, software and video copying are...

a) $3 million
b) $90 million
c) $6,000 million

(answers on page 32)

NEW CRIME BOOM

One of the biggest crime problems today are so-called 'white-collar' crimes. Most of these are crimes committed by employees to give the companies they work for an unfair advantage over rival firms – for example, by illegal price-fixing, fraud or industrial espionage. It is estimated that in the USA alone, white-collar crime is worth around $200 billion every year – ten times the cost of all the burglaries, thefts and robberies put together!

ARMCHAIR DETECTIVES

In many countries, television programmes enable viewers at home to help detectives solve real-life crimes. These programmes show crime reconstructions (where actors play the parts of criminals), stolen or missing property and pictures of people the police would like to interview. Viewers can then phone in with any useful information they have.

Modern private eyes

PRIVATE EYES, PRIVATE SPIES

Private investigators also play a major part in modern law enforcement. Often, they are hired to track down people who have gone into hiding to avoid giving evidence in court. Their work also includes finding kidnap victims, searching for missing people, surveillance and helping companies to detect dishonest employees.

DETECTIVES TODAY

Today's detectives must learn new skills to tackle new types of crime. Meanwhile, ordinary people can play their part in bringing outlaws to justice – by watching television.

Fast-paced detection

ROBO-COPS

The fastest crime-busters today are computers – they match fingerprints found at a crime scene at a rate of 60,000 per second!

WATCH OUT!

Private eyes, undercover police officers and secret agents are secretly at work all around us. So keep your eyes peeled – you never know who might be watching you!

Index

Quiz answers

- **Page 2** a, Sean Connery; b, David Niven; c, 7.
- **Page 4** b, sneakies; c, compasses; b, pinhole cameras.
- **Page 6** b, Holland; b, US Civil War; a, L'Alouette.
- **Page 8** c, Nighthawk; c, to stop their blood from boiling; a, Early Bird.
- **Page 10** c, E; b, the decoding of messages; a, the telegraph.
- **Page 12** b, The Black Cabinet; c, The Scarlet Pimpernel; a, pigeon.
- **Page 14** b, Sidney Reilly; a, Allan Pinkerton; b, Kim.

- **Page 17** c, MI5; a, J. Edgar Hoover; a, Military Intelligence.
- **Page 18** c, 177; b, after the Second World War; b, Lyon.
- **Page 20** c, Kevin Costner; a, Scarface; b, Peelers.
- **Page 22** b, Inspector Maigret; c, Peter Sellers; a, Belgian.
- **Page 25** b, an Alsatian; a, canine teams; c, Scooby Doo.
- **Page 26** b, 4; a, double helix; c, whorl.
- **Page 29** b, an autopsy; c, Crimewatch UK; a, Dr. Crippen.
- **Page 30** b, a device for keeping calls private; a, piracy; c, $6,000 million.

Acknowledgements

Copyright © 2006 **ticktock** Entertainment Ltd. First published in Great Britain by ticktock Media Ltd.,
Unit 2, Orchard Business Centre, North Farm Road, Tunbridge Wells, Kent TN2 3XF, Great Britain.
All rights reserved. No part of this publication may be reproduced, stored in a retrieval system, or transmitted in any form or by any means electronic, mechanical, photocopying, recording or otherwise, without prior written permission of the copyright owner.
A CIP catalogue record for this book is available from the British Library.
ISBN 1 86007 960 1 Printed in China.
Picture Credits: t = top, b = bottom, c = centre, l = left, r=right, OFC = outside front cover, OBC = outside back cover, IFC = inside front cover
Ann Ronan @ Image Select; 8/9t. Corbis; 4/5, 7, 16/17, 17r, 19t, 20t, 21b, 24/25 & IFC, 25t, 27b, 28/29t, 28/29b, 30b. Imperial War Museum; 9b. P.OTHONIEL GAMMA; 14/15.
Science Photo Library; 10/11. Stone-UK Press; 5. Telegraph Colour Library; 19b, 26/27, 30/31. The Kobal Collection; 2, 2/3, 22b, 23. Topham Picture Point; 6/7. Tony Stone; 14l.